To Elodie, Felicity, and Tim—come rain or
shine, we'll always find rainbows together.

—R.D.

To my wonderful parents.

—W.T.

This edition published in 2023 by Flying Eye Books Ltd.
27 Westgate Street, London, E8 3RL

Text © Rachael Davis 2023
Illustrations © Wenjia Tang 2023

Every attempt has been made to ensure any statements written as fact have been checked
to the best of our abilities. However, we are still human, thankfully, and occasionally little
mistakes may crop up. Should you spot any errors, please email info@nobrow.net.

Edited by Sara Forster
Designed by Ivanna Khomyak
Science consultant James Doyle

1 3 5 7 9 10 8 6 4 2

Published by Flying Eye Books Ltd.
Printed in Poland on FSC® certified paper.

ISBN: 978-1-838748-57-9

Order from www.flyingeyebooks.com

Rachael Davis • Wenjia Tang

OVER THE RAINBOW

The Science, Magic, and Meaning of Rainbows

Flying Eye Books

Contents

THE SYMBOL OF THE RAINBOW

Introduction

Have you ever looked at the sky on a sunny, rainy day and seen a magnificent curve of beautiful colors? You're looking right at a rainbow! These natural wonders have dazzled humankind for thousands of years, and over time scientists have uncovered the secrets of how they are formed. But the rainbow is much more than just a scientific marvel...

This book looks not only at the science behind rainbows, but also at their place in mythology, cultural beliefs, and politics, as well as at some of the magical ways rainbows have inspired great works of art, music, and storytelling. No matter the weather, the symbol of the rainbow continues to be used all over the world as a sign of unity, peace, and hope.

THE SCIENCE OF RAINBOWS

On a sunny but rainy day, you might see a rainbow in the sky, but how does sunlight and clear water create a band of brilliant colors?

A Close Look at Light

To discover how rainbows are made, you need to know some cool facts about light.

Quick as a flash

Light is a kind of energy that makes it possible for us to see the world around us. Most light comes from the Sun, but electric light bulbs, lightning, and flames give off light, too. You can't see it moving, but light is the fastest thing that exists. It travels at 186,000 mi per second! Flick a switch on a dark night, and light instantly fills the room.

Light and shade

Because light travels in straight lines, if light shines on an object that isn't see-through, it can't pass through it or bend around it. The light is blocked and a shadow is made.

Flying colors!

Light looks white, but it is actually made up of seven colors mixed together: red, orange, yellow, green, blue, indigo (purply blue), and violet.

Traveling light

Each of the colors in light has its own wavy pattern, with a different length between the waves' peaks. This is called its wavelength. Red has the longest wavelength, followed by orange, yellow, green, blue, indigo, and then violet with the shortest wavelength. This is why the colored bands in a rainbow always appear in the same order.

DID YOU KNOW?

We often say "light travels in straight lines." In fact, light travels in wiggly waves. It is these light waves that travel in straight lines.

Really Old Yaks Go By In Vans.

Rinse Out Your Granny's Boots In Vinegar.

Richard Of York Gave Battle In Vain.

Silly sentences

The easiest way to remember the order of the colors in the rainbow is to say a sentence with words that start with the first letter of each color.

Reflection, Refraction, and Dispersion

Although light can only travel in straight lines, scientists have uncovered how it bounces, bends, and even spreads apart. Light has to do all three in order to make a rainbow.

Light and sight

When we see an object, we are actually seeing the light that reflects off it. We see colors because objects only reflect some of the light. This apple looks red because it reflects red light. The orange, yellow, green, blue, indigo, and violet light is absorbed by the apple.

Bending light

A piece of triangular glass called a prism can bend and split white light into a spectrum—the name given to all of light's different colors. When light enters the prism, it bends (this is called refraction)and spreads apart (this is called dispersion). A rainbow of colors shines out of the other side of the prism.

DID YOU KNOW?

Our amazing eyes can detect millions of different shades of color.

Refraction in action!

You can see refraction, or the bendy effect of light, simply with a pencil and some water. Light travels through water and air at different speeds and in different directions, so when you look at a pencil in a bowl of water, it appears to be bent!

The long and short of it

When light enters a water droplet, it bends and splits into its different colors. Each colored wavelength bends at a slightly different angle. The colors with short wavelengths bend the most and the colors with longer wavelengths bend the least—which is why red light appears at the top of the rainbow and violet at the bottom.

Making Rainbows

Take millions of tiny raindrops falling from the sky, add a beam of sunshine, and what do you get? A rainbow! It's not magic, but the science of bendy, bouncy light.

Bend and spread...

Raindrops act like tiny prisms. When sunlight shines into a water droplet, the light bends as it moves from the air into the water. This is refraction, and the light now spreads out into all of its colors. This is dispersion.

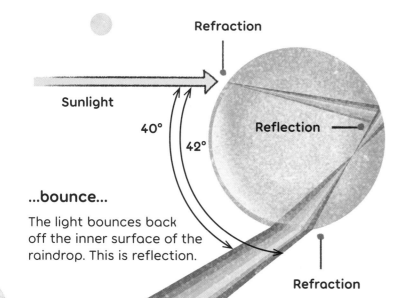

...bounce...

The light bounces back off the inner surface of the raindrop. This is reflection.

...and bend again

When the light leaves the water droplet, it refracts (bends) again as it travels back into the air. For anyone looking in the right place at the right time, this reflected, scattered light will create a rainbow.

DID YOU KNOW?

Blue-violet light exits the water droplet at an angle of around 40 degrees, while red light exits at around 42 degrees. The steeper angle of the red light makes it appear at the top of the rainbow to the observer.

TOP TIP:

Remember, light travels in and out of the same side of the water droplets, so if you want to see a rainbow, make sure the sun is behind you and the raindrops are in front of you.

16

Sunlight

DID YOU KNOW?

Raindrops are usually shaped like spheres, not teardrops. Their round shape allows the light to bend and bounce back to create a rainbow.

Ancient Ideas

Rainbows were a mystery for thousands of years. It took some of the ancient world's brightest brains to slowly uncover the rainbow's secrets.

[c.400 BCE] The first theory of the rainbow

Aristotle was a great thinker who lived in Greece over 2,000 years ago. He studied many subjects and came up with theories to explain the world around him.

He discovered that rainbows only occurred when water droplets were in the air. However, he wrongly believed they were formed by the reflection of the sun in clouds. He also thought rainbows only had three colors: red, green, and violet.

King Ptolemy II of Egypt, who ruled in 283–246 BCE, bought lots of Aristotle's books, and Aristotle's rainbow theory spread across the Middle East.

DID YOU KNOW?

Aristotle is believed to have come up with the first theory of color. He thought that all colors came from white and black (lightness and darkness) and that they were sent by God through rays of heavenly light. Aristotle's theory was widely accepted until Sir Isaac Newton showed how to split light through a prism.

[800s–1200s] Discoveries in the Middle East

Syrian scientist Ayyub al-Ruhawi (Job of Edessa) challenged Aristotle's theory that rainbows only formed when there are clouds, but he still believed they were made of three colors.

Later, Persian scientist Ibn-Sina (Avicenna) realized that rainbows formed in water spray. Then Arab mathematician and scientist Ibn al-Haytham (Alhazen) became the first person to describe refraction—the way that light can bend and change direction.

Finally, the Persian thinker Qutb al-Din al-Shirazi claimed that a rainbow formed when light was refracted (bent) and reflected inside a raindrop. Hooray! Unfortunately, Qutb's work didn't reach the Western world for a very long time!

DID YOU KNOW?

Aristotle and Ibn-Sina's work only became widely known in the Western world when the Spanish conquered the Arabian-ruled city of Toledo in the 11th century and discovered a huge library of books with theories about rainbows.

Solving the Riddle of the Rainbow

Over time, great thinkers and scientists in the Western world set out to prove their theories about rainbows with colorful experiments.

Giant raindrops

In 1304, German thinker and scientist Theodoric of Freiberg set out to prove his theory that each raindrop was capable of producing a rainbow. He created a giant raindrop using a round flask filled with water. He placed it in a dark room and directed a beam of sunlight at it, which created the rainbow just as he had predicted. He proved that the raindrop acts like a mirror, reflecting light.

DID YOU KNOW?

German scientist Johannes Kepler also discovered the Law of Refraction around the same time. But no one knew because it was only explained in private letters! Kepler compared the colors in the rainbow to an octave of musical notes.

Cracking the theory

In 1637, French scientist René Descartes used math and newly invented tools and instruments to measure the angle of light entering a raindrop. He was able to figure out the Law of Refraction and showed that rays that enter a droplet are reflected back once from the inner surface at specific angles.

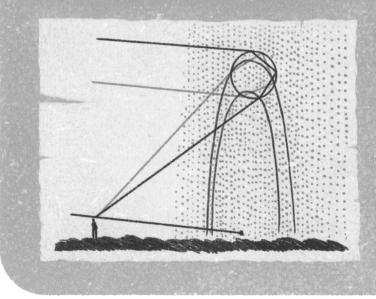

Light isn't white

In 1666, the famous scientist Sir Isaac Newton carried out experiments to prove that white light consists of many colors. Newton directed a beam of light into a prism, which spread the white light into its seven colors. Newton was the first person to use the word "spectrum" to describe the rainbow of colors.

At that time, some scientists believed that light was white and that the colors were caused by the water or glass that the light passed through.

To prove that the colors were naturally present in light, Newton set up another experiment. He directed light into a second prism, which concentrated the rays back together and produced white light again.

RARE RAINBOWS

Rainbows can form anywhere there is moisture in the air, including splashing waterfalls and sea spray—and even the cloud of damp air that bursts out of a whale's blowhole!

Rainbow Wow!

What's better than seeing a rainbow in the sky? Seeing more than one at once! These rare and spectacular sights only happen when the weather conditions are just right...

Seeing double

Double rainbows appear when the light is reflected twice inside the same raindrop. The **primary** (lower) rainbow is created by the first reflection. The **secondary** (upper) rainbow is created by the second reflection.

It's twins!

Twinned rainbows have two arcs that start from the same base. The order of the colors is the same in both arcs. They occur when two rain showers with different-sized raindrops mix together.

Spot the difference!

Reflecting the light twice means the colors in the secondary rainbow are flipped, with red on the inside and purple on the outside.

Secondary rainbow

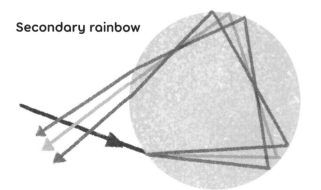

Raining hamburgers

Raindrops flatten as they fall through the air. Larger, heavier raindrops flatten more, so they end up shaped like hamburgers. Light travels out of the different-shaped droplets in two different directions, creating an extra rainbow.

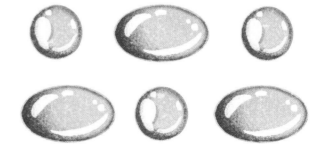

Reflection rainbow

If direct rays of light reflect back off the surface of a body of water and then pass through water droplets in the air, a reflection rainbow will appear.

Primary rainbow

Secondary rainbow

Reflection primary rainbow

Reflected secondary rainbow

Reflected reflection primary rainbow

Reflected primary rainbow

Reflected rainbow

This is NOT a reflection of a rainbow, as you might think. Reflected rainbows appear on the surface of rivers and lakes when rays of light pass through rain droplets and then reflect off the water.

Unusual Rainbows

Usually, rainbows appear in the sky as a beautiful arc made up of seven colors, but in some unusual weather conditions, we might see more or fewer colors, or even a dazzling full circle!

Red alert!

At sunset and sunrise, when the sun is low in the sky and there is rain around, something magical can happen. Turn your back on the sun and face the rain, and you might be lucky enough to see a **red rainbow**. These fiery-colored rainbows are caused by the way sunlight travels through the air that surrounds Earth (called the atmosphere). It's the reason for red sunrises and sunsets, too.

Why are sunsets red?

When the sun is low, short, wiggly waves of blue and green light scatter during the long journey through the atmosphere. Long, wavy waves of red light travel more directly, so the sky looks red—and if it rains, so do rainbows.

Why is the sky blue?

When the sun is high in the sky, its light has a shorter distance to travel through Earth's atmosphere. The short, wiggly waves of blue light scatter in all directions, making the sky look blue.

Sunrise/Sunset

Midday

Super rainbows

Rainbows with extra bands of color on the inside are called **supernumerary rainbows**. The pastel shades of purple, pink, and green are formed by small, almost identically sized raindrops.

Going round in circles

A **full-circle rainbow** is a dazzling, rare sight. Every rainbow is a circle, but most of the time we only see part of it because the rest is blocked by the ground. However, with the right conditions, you could see a full circle—the lower the sun is in the sky, the more of the rainbow you will see.

DID YOU KNOW?

An airplane pilot flying high in the sky has the best chance of spotting a full-circle rainbow because there is no ground to block the view.

Almost Rainbows

We know that a rainbow occurs when sunlight travels through water droplets. But what happens if a different type of light travels through a different kind of droplet?

It's all a bit hazy

A **white rainbow**, or **fogbow**, is created when light travels through mist or fog. Fog is made up of tiny water droplets that hang in the air. Sunlight goes through a process called diffraction which makes the reflected light spread out, so the colors in a fogbow are not as strong and often appear to be white.

On top of the world

Glories look like a circular rainbow and are usually seen by pilots or mountaineers. This is because glories can only be seen when light passes through mist or clouds that are below the observer. Glories occur in a direct line with the sun, which must be behind the observer.

CAN RAINBOWS FORM IN SPACE?

In 2018, a German astronaut, Alexander Gerst, witnessed a glory from space.

A lunar rainbow (or moonbow)

If you are stood with the moon behind you and a rain shower in front of you, it is possible you may see a **lunar rainbow** form.

DID YOU KNOW?

If moonlight travels through fog, you get a lunar fogbow! This is incredibly rare, and the moonlight has to be very strong for a lunar fogbow to appear.

Sparkling rings

On freezing-cold, clear days, moisture in the air turns to tiny ice crystals. When sunlight shines through the frozen specks, a white ring, called a **halo**, is produced around the hazy sun.

Upside-down bow

This is actually a type of halo called a **circumzenithal arc**. They often form when sunlight travels through high, wispy clouds made of hexagonal ice crystals.

RAINBOW MYTHS AND LEGENDS

A rainbow in the morning is the sailor's warning.

A rainbow at night is the shepherd's delight.

Weather lore is a collection of proverbs and informal folklore that relate to predicting the weather and certain weather signals. There are several proverbs about the rainbow that date back centuries.

How it All Began

Our quest to unlock the secrets of the rainbow goes far beyond science. Since ancient times, rainbows have appeared in mythology and religious texts, often connected to the heavens.

Mending a hole in the sky

In Chinese mythology, Nüwa (女娲) is often described as a female with the body of a snake and a human head. It is said that as Nüwa wandered the natural world, she felt lonely, so she created animals and humans. At this time, the heavens were being held up above the Earth by great pillars. When a fight between the god of water and the god of fire destroyed one of the pillars, tearing a hole in the sky, Nüwa came to humankind's rescue. She melted down five colored stones and used them to seal the sky.

The Floating Bridge of Heaven

In the ancient Japanese story of creation, two of the heavenly deities, Izanagi and Izaami, were ordered to create land on the Earth. They stood upon the Floating Bridge of Heaven (Ame no Uki Hashi), traditionally believed to be a rainbow, and used a jeweled spear to stir the oily ocean below Heaven until it grew thick. As they pulled the spear out, liquid dripped down and piled up to form the first island on Earth, called Onogoro. Then Izanagi and Izaami traveled down the rainbow bridge from Heaven to Earth.

DID YOU KNOW?

Japan's deep connection to the rainbow bridge continues to this day. In 1993, Japan opened the Rainbow Bridge that crosses northern Tokyo Bay. The wires of the suspension bridge contain solar-powered lights that illuminate the night sky.

The Rainbow Goddess

In ancient Greek mythology, Iris was the goddess of the rainbow and the messenger of the gods. There are no specific mythological stories centered around Iris, but like a rainbow in the sky, she appears from time to time.

Messenger to the gods

The name Iris (Ἶρις) means "the rainbow" in ancient Greek and originates from *erô eirô* meaning "the speaker" or "messenger." She was described by some writers, like the Roman poet Ovid, as traveling along the rainbow, delivering messages. Alongside this task, the Greek poet Hesiod said Iris was also responsible for delivering water from the River Styx in a large jug called a ewer, whenever a god had to take an oath. If a god drank the water and lied, it would knock them unconscious for a year!

A work of art

The ancient Greeks didn't just tell the stories of the gods, they also depicted them in art. On surviving ancient Greek vases, Iris is often shown with wings, holding a ewer in her hands. In the 5th century BCE, the Greek sculptor Pheidias decorated the Parthenon temple on the Acropolis in Athens with marble statues of Greek gods. He included Iris on the west pediment between Athena and Poseidon.

DID YOU KNOW?

The word "iridescent," meaning bright colors that appear to change when seen from different angles, is derived from the Greek work for rainbow—"iris."

Bifröst

In Norse mythology, Bifröst is a rainbow bridge that connects Asgard, the world of the gods, to Midgard, the world of humanity.

The rainbow bridge

Some people think the Old Norse word Bifröst means "the shaking or trembling rainbow," while others claim it means "shimmering path" or "the swaying road to Heaven." But in the earlier myths, the bridge was referred to as Bilröst, meaning "the fleetingly glimpsed rainbow."

DID YOU KNOW?

Bifröst is guarded by Heimdall, the watchman of the gods.

The Rainbow Serpent

Aboriginal Australians were the first people of Australia, and the elders have passed down stories of the Dreamtime for centuries. One of their shared Dreamtime ancestral beings is the immortal rainbow serpent. It has many names, and the stories vary by tribe and region of Australia.

The giver and taker of life

The rainbow serpent is often seen as the giver and taker of life, linked with water and the weather. Some stories say that the rainbow serpent brought water to the Earth, creating rivers and life, and then went to rest. There are cautionary tales, too. The rainbow serpent should not be angered and will punish those who do wrong. Some say the rainbow serpent is resting in a waterhole and shouldn't be disturbed. When it rains, the rainbow serpent moves across the sky from one waterhole to another, creating a colored bow in the sky, the rainbow.

DID YOU KNOW?

Aboriginal rock art of the rainbow serpent has been discovered that was made around 6,000 years ago. This makes the rainbow serpent one of the world's oldest surviving beliefs.

The power of stories

The Dreamtime stories are passed down the generations, not only through oral tales but also through art. Aboriginal Australians would carve and paint on rock using ochre, a natural earth pigment that comes in a variety of colors, from yellow and orange to brown. The tribes did not have a written language, so their art and use of symbols was an essential form of communication and continues to be a way to pass down their cultural heritage.

DID YOU KNOW?

Until recently, these sacred stories of the Aboriginal tribes were not shared with the wider world. Even now, it is often only senior members, or elders of the tribes, who are allowed to tell or paint their stories.

The Leprechaun's Pot of Gold

In modern-day Irish folklore, it is said that a leprechaun hides a pot of gold at the end of a rainbow. But strangely, while the myth of the Irish leprechaun has been around for hundreds of years, their connection to rainbows has not.

What is folklore?

Folklore is the collection of stories and cultural beliefs of a group of people that have been passed down from generation to generation by word of mouth. This means that the stories often evolve over time and there is not always a written record of such traditions.

William Butler Yeats (1865–1939)

The Irish poet and Nobel Prize winner W.B. Yeats was fascinated by Irish folklore. In his book *Irish Fairy and Folk Tales*, he wrote that if someone were to catch a leprechaun, they could make him give them "crocks" (pots) of gold, but warned that if you took your eyes off him, he would vanish like smoke. This is believed to have inspired today's modern story of the leprechaun hiding his pot of gold at the end of the rainbow.

DID YOU KNOW?

If someone is trying to achieve something that seems impossible, people may say they are "chasing rainbows."

The Irish leprechaun

When leprechauns first appeared in stories around the 8th century, they were called "luchorpán." Tales of these mischievous tricksters and their appearance have taken shape over time. They were often described as old, bearded men, wearing a red or green jacket, a pointy hat, and buckled shoes, and were usually shoemakers!

A modern-day tale

One day, a farmer caught a leprechaun, who claimed to have hidden a pot of gold at the end of the rainbow. The farmer searched and searched, but he never found the gold because it was a trick! A rainbow is an image, not an object, so the end of the rainbow doesn't exist! They are also full circles, and so have no ends!

RAINBOWS
IN THE ARTS

"Rainbow" by artist Marcus Canning is made up of nine brightly colored recycled shipping containers. The sculpture overlooks Fremantle Port near Perth, Western Australia.

Once Upon a Time

Rainbows have not only dazzled in the sky, but also in the pages of books, plays, poems, and even fairy tales.

Lang's colorful fairy tales

Scottish writer Andrew Lang (1844–1912) compiled over 400 fairy tales written by different authors into a series of 12 books. Each "Fairy Book" was named after a different color. In Lang's *Yellow Fairy Book* is one particularly colorful fairy tale featuring Prince Rainbow, called "Fairer-than-a-Fairy." It was written in 1698 by French novelist Charlotte-Rose de Caumont de La Force (1646-1724).

DID YOU KNOW?

La Force is best known for writing the fairy tale "Persinette" which was adapted by Brothers Grimm into the popular fairy tale... "Rapunzel!"

A rainbow fairy tale

When a kind king finally had a child, he thought she was so beautiful, he named her "Fairer-than-a-Fairy," but this angered the fairies. A wicked fairy locked the princess away in a distant palace. One sunny day, when the princess passed a fountain in the palace gardens, a brilliant rainbow formed. To her surprise, the rainbow started talking to her! The rainbow introduced himself as Prince Rainbow. He told her how the fairies had captured him a long time ago and put him into a deep sleep so that now he could only appear in the world as a rainbow.

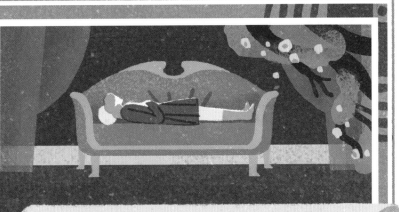

Fairer-than-a-Fairy and Prince Rainbow would meet every time the sun shone on the water in just the right way to form a rainbow, and soon fell in love. The princess escaped from the wicked fairy and set off through the woods to look for Prince Rainbow. Eventually, she came to a castle. Inside, she discovered a large room with rainbow-colored curtains draped around a couch. On the couch lay Prince Rainbow in his human form in a deep sleep. It wasn't easy, but Fairer-than-a-Fairy awoke Prince Rainbow, and they lived happily ever after.

Over the Rainbow

Some of the most famous songs featuring rainbows are found in cinema, from Arthur Hamilton's "I Can Sing a Rainbow" in the film *Pete Kelly's Blues* to Kermit the Frog's classic performance of "Rainbow Connection" in *The Muppet Movie*. Perhaps the most famous rainbow song of all comes from a well-known film about a girl who follows a yellow brick road...

The Wizard of Oz

When Dorothy is caught in a tornado, she wakes up in the magical Land of Oz. With the help of a cowardly lion, a brainless scarecrow, and a heartless tin man, Dorothy travels along the yellow brick road to meet the Wizard of Oz and return home. At the start of the film, young Dorothy is dreaming of a place where you could never get into any trouble. She decides that if such a wonderful place exists, it must be somewhere over the rainbow.

Over the rainbow

Actress Judy Garland is famously known for singing "Over the Rainbow" when she starred as Dorothy Gale in the 1939 film *The Wizard of Oz* (based on the children's book by L. Frank Baum). Composed by Harold Arlen with lyrics by Edgar Harburg, the song went on to win an Academy Award for Best Original Song.

DID YOU KNOW?

To emphasize the all-important first word of the song, "somewhere," Arlen composed the first two notes to be exactly an octave (eight notes) apart. This means that "some" and "where" both have the same musical note (A), but the second A is an octave higher in pitch!

DID YOU KNOW?

"Over the Rainbow" has been performed by lots of different musicians, including American singer Eva Cassidy and Israel Ka'ano'i Kamakawiwo'ole, a musician from Hawaii who performed his version with a ukulele.

47

I Can See a Rainbow

Throughout history, artists have celebrated the rainbow as a natural wonder, as well as used it to express a significant meaning or message.

"Arundel Castle on the River Arun, with a Rainbow"

During the Romantic period, around 1824, British artist J.M.W. Turner (1775–1851) created a watercolor painting of Arundel Castle with a large rainbow in the sky. The science of the rainbow was a hot topic at this time, and Turner had many discussions about the colors of light with his friends. Romantic artists and poets thought that advances in science took away from the natural beauty and mystery of the world.

"Rainbow Portrait"

In "Rainbow Portrait," the Tudor queen Elizabeth I is seen holding a bow inscribed with the words "non sine sole iris," which means "no rainbow without the sun." The sun was a symbol of a monarch's divine right to rule, and the rainbow was a sign of peace. Together, they symbolized Elizabeth's reign of peace and prosperity.

Elements of art: "Colour"

Swiss-born artist Angelica Kauffmann (1741–1807) became a founding member of the Royal Academy of Art. In "Colour," she depicts a female artist reaching up with her paintbrush to collect the colors of a rainbow.

Rainbow Village

Huang Yung-fu was born in China in 1922 and served in the military until he was forced to flee to Taiwan in 1949. He was temporarily housed in a military village, but this later became permanent. When Yung-fu was 86, the government announced its plans to demolish the village, but Yung-fu didn't want to leave. So he picked up a brush and painted a small bird on the wall of his two-bedroom bungalow. He painted and painted until the village was covered in his vibrant artwork, from the pavements to the rooftops. News began to spread, and he became known as "Rainbow Grandpa." In 2010, the Taiwanese government confirmed it would preserve Rainbow Village as a public park.

THE SYMBOL OF THE RAINBOW

During the COVID-19 global pandemic, many children across Europe made "lockdown rainbows" to display in their windows to show support for the key workers who were helping people stay safe and well.

Watch Out for the Rainbow

Look out! In different cultures, mythologies, and religions, rainbows are often thought to be omens—a sign or warning that something good or bad might happen in the future...

A good omen...

In the Old Testament of the Christian Bible, rainbows are seen as a good omen. When God saw the greed of humankind, he ordered Noah to build an ark before a great flood. Noah and his family boarded the ark along with two of each species of animal. Then God made it rain for forty days and forty nights, flooding the Earth. A long time passed, and Noah sent out a dove to check for dry land. When the dove brought back an olive branch, Noah knew it was safe to leave the ark. God promised Noah that He would not destroy the Earth with a flood again and cast a rainbow as a reassuring sign of His promise.

A bad omen...

In Amazonian culture, rainbows are considered to be bad omens. Many believe that the spirits of the rainbow could cause harm to children and pregnant women. This widespread belief started in the pre-Incan civilization in Peru (900–200 BCE), where people would close their mouths when they saw a rainbow, to avoid disease entering the body. In Amuesha, a language spoken in central Peru, there is a disease called ayona'achartan which translates as "the rainbow hurt my skin."

Flags Through History

Throughout history, rainbows have been used on flags all over the world. But what is the meaning behind these colorful flags, flapping in the wind?

The Buddhist flag

First used in 1885 in Sri Lanka, the rainbow flag is a symbol of peace and faith. When the World Fellowship of Buddhists (WFB) was formed in 1950, the five-colored flag became the international Buddhist flag. It is now recognized by Buddhists all over the world.

The peace movement

The rainbow flag was used in the 1961 Peace March in Italy. It featured the Italian word "PACE," which means "peace." Since then, the flag has been used across the world as a symbol of peace on International Peace Day (September 21).

Pride

In 1978, the rainbow flag became a symbol of hope and diversity in the LGBTQ+ community. It originally had eight stripes, but pink and turquoise were removed. This left the remaining six colors: red (for life), orange (for healing), yellow (for sunlight), green (for nature), blue (for harmony), and violet (for spirit).

The rainbow nation

In 1994, after South Africa's first democratic election, Archbishop Desmond Tutu nicknamed the country the "Rainbow Nation." He had fought for equality between racial ethnicities. On 27 April 1994, a new, six-colored flag was lifted, to represent all segments of society in South Africa.

New Zealand's Rainbow Warrior

Founded in 1971, Greenpeace is a non-violent independent organization that actively fights to protect the environment. The *Rainbow Warrior* ship was the flagship of the Greenpeace fleet. On 10 July 1985, the *Rainbow Warrior* was planning to travel in protest of French nuclear weapons testing. However, it was bombed and sunk by the French intelligence services, killing one crew member. In 1988–1990, a memorial sculpture for the *Rainbow Warrior* was established in Matauri Bay, New Zealand.

GREENPEACE

Standing Proud

The rainbow is an important symbol for the LGBTQ+ community. They have had to fight for equality and their right to love who they choose, and to be accepted for who they are.

Taking a stand

In the 1960s, many bars in the USA refused to serve LGBTQ+ people. The Stonewall Inn in New York was a bar where it was safe for LGBTQ+ people to socialize. But on 28 June 1969, the police raided the Stonewall Inn and began to arrest people for no reason other than their sexuality. The people in the bar were tired of being unfairly treated and threw bottles and cut the tyres of the police cars. It turned into a riot. For the rest of that week, the LGBTQ+ community protested on the streets for the right to be treated fairly. The Gay Liberation Front (GLF) was formed to continue to actively fight for equality.

Making a sign

In 1977, Harvey Milk became one of the first openly gay politically elected officials in the USA. He commissioned Gilbert Baker to design a symbol of hope and diversity for the LGBTQ+ community. In 1978, the rainbow flag was adopted.

Never forgetting

The rainbow flag continues to be an important symbol and a reminder of the community's history. Each year, they come together on the anniversary of the Stonewall riot for PRIDE parades and marches all around the world. June is recognized as PRIDE month. For the 2015 celebration of PRIDE in the UK, the London Eye was lit with the colors of the rainbow.

Marching on

Today, the LGBTQ+ community still have to fight for their right to be treated fairly. It wasn't until 2014 in the UK and 2015 in the USA that gay marriage was legalized. To celebrate the US Supreme Court legalizing gay marriage in all 50 states of America, the White House was lit up in rainbow colors.

Conclusion

What do rainbows mean to you? There is no right or wrong answer! These stunning bows of color mean so many things to different people all over the world. Scientists have rejoiced in uncovering the way light reflects and refracts through water droplets, while artists have tried to capture the rainbow's beauty in paintings and stories. Magical, mythical, and meaningful tales of the rainbow have been passed down through generations, from the legends of the rainbow bridge Bifröst to the warnings of the Amazonians.

So the next time you see a rainbow, will you spy the rainbow serpent moving from its waterhole? Will you go looking for the leprechaun's pot of gold? Will you feel the urge to sing one of your favorite rainbow songs, or will you think about the people who have used the symbol of the rainbow as a sign of unity, peace, and hope?

Whatever you do, one thing is for sure; rainbows are a natural wonder of the world, and what they mean to us will continue to evolve and grow over time.

Glossary

Aboriginal – the first native people of a land

Atmosphere – a layer of gases surrounding the planet

Compose – to write or create a work of art, like a piece of music or poetry

COVID-19 – an infectious disease caused by coronavirus which spreads through the air when people cough or sneeze

Deity – a god or goddess

Diffracton – the spreading of waves around an object or an obstacle

Dispersion – the splitting of white light into the seven colors of the visible spectrum

Dreamtime – the beginning of time, when Aboriginal Australians believe their ancestors created the world

Folklore – the collection of stories and cultural beliefs of a group of people that have been passed down from generation to generation by word of mouth

Greenpeace – a non-violent independent organization that actively fights to protect the environment, founded in 1971

Hexagon – a shape with six sides

Illuminate – to light up a place or a street with lights

Immortal – someone (or something) who lives for ever and never dies

Iridescent – bright colors that appear to change when seen from different angles

Leprechaun – a small, magical creature from Irish folklore often portrayed as a trickster

Lore – knowledge or information passed on from person to person

Index

Lunar – something related to the moon

Memorial – a statue or structure established to remind people of a person or event

Octave – the interval between one musical note and the next note of the same name above or below it

Omen – something that is considered to be a sign or warning that something good or bad might happen in the future

Pandemic – when an infectious disease becomes widespread worldwide, affecting many people

Pediment – the upper triangular front of a classical building, usually above pillars

Prism – a 3-dimensional shape which has a constant cross-section and both ends are the same shape

Proverb – a short, well-known saying that states a truth or gives advice

Reflection – a process in which light returns back from a surface

Refraction – a process in which a ray of light bends and changes direction

Riot – people behaving violently in a public place

Romantic – a term used to describe art, music, and literature from the late 18th century to the early 19th century which expressed mankind's emotional connection to nature

Spectrum – a band of colors like those in a rainbow

Supernumerary – when there is more of something present than normal, for example, more colors in the rainbow than normal

Ukulele – a small, four-string guitar, originally from Hawaii

Wavelength – the distance between wave peaks